He Is
Risen

He Is Risen

compiled by
Bonnie Harvey

BARBOUR
PUBLISHING, INC.
Uhrichsville, Ohio

Barbour Publishing, Inc. expresses its appreciation to those who generously gave permission
to reprint copyrighted material. Diligent effort has been made to identify, locate, contact, and
secure permission to use copyrighted material. If any permissions or acknowledgments have
been inadvertently omitted or if such permissions were not received by the time of publica-
tion, the publisher would sincerely appreciate receiving complete information so that correct
credit can be given in future editions. "A Prayer for the Transforming of Everyday Life" by
Peter Marshall. Taken from *The Prayers of Peter Marshall* by Catherine Marshall. Published
by Fleming H. Revell, a division of Baker Book House, Grand Rapids, MI 49516. Used by
permission. "One Easter" by Sharon Banigan. Taken from *Prayers and Graces: Dennis the
Menace* by Hank Ketcham. Published by Westminster/John Knox Press, Louisville, KY
40202.

ISBN 1-57748-430-4

All Scripture quotations (unless otherwise noted) are taken
from the Authorized King James Version of the Bible.

Scripture quotations marked NIV are taken from the *Holy Bible,
New International Version®, NIV®,* © 1973, 1978, 1984 by the
International Bible Society. Used by permission of Zondervan
Publishing House. All rights reserved.

Published by Barbour Publishing, Inc., P.O. Box 719
Uhrichsville, Ohio 44683 http://www.barbourbooks.com

Member of the
Evangelical Christian
Publishers Association

Printed in the United States of America.

CONTENTS

"He is risen, indeed!"

The joyous conviction expressed in this greeting—once exchanged by the early Christians—reverberates today. Because the Resurrection is the very embodiment of our hope, the Easter season is the highlight of the Christian calendar.

The Resurrection established that Jesus is the Son of God: the fulfillment of all prophecy, the Sacrifice for all sin, and the King for all eternity.

As this significant season approaches, spend some time in silent reflection and prayer.

Then. . .sense the awe. Anticipate the hope. Experience the joy.

FAMILY
EASTER
ACTIVITIES

The dauntless crocuses poke their emerald tips through the last of the winter's snows, and the saffron daffodils sway in the chilly breeze. Glorious forsythia bushes dot the greening lawns, and bold tulips splash their varied colors in carefully tended beds. Rosebush stems bulge with the promise of their first buds. After the long dreariness of winter, our spirits are refreshed by the kaleidoscope of colors displayed among the spring flowers. Yet for the gardener— more than anyone else—this time has unusual significance. The gardener has planted, cultivated, and nurtured, and now waits expectantly for the first signs of life. The enjoyment derived depends upon the effort expended.

And so it is with the enjoyment of the Easter season. While Easter is an "internal," or spiritual, holiday, external preparation can enhance our internal appreciation. Special seasonal activities with our families, a few pertinent read-aloud stories, a kitchen adventure with several new recipes, and discussions that clarify the traditions we follow can quicken our spirits to perceive the true meaning of Easter in a refreshing way.

ACTIVITY TIME

As Passion Week, or Holy Week, begins, the family can be involved in this activity to focus their minds on the real meaning of Easter. On small slips of paper, write Scripture references (one reference per slip) that correspond to each day's event throughout Holy Week. Place each slip in a plastic Easter egg, and place the eggs in a decorated basket. Just before or after a meal together, members can take turns selecting an egg and reading aloud the designated verses.

Some Suggested Verses:

Palm Sunday: Preparation for Jerusalem entry—
Matthew 21:1–9
Protest by the Pharisees—
Luke 19:37–40
Triumphal entry into Jerusalem—
Matthew 21:10–16
Return to Bethany—
Matthew 21:17

Monday: The fig tree cursed—
Mark 11:13–14
Cleansing of the temple—
Mark 11:15–17
The plot against Jesus—
Luke 19:47–48

	Jesus outside the city—
	Luke 21:37–38
Tuesday:	The withered fig tree—
	Mark 11:20–22
	Jesus and John the Baptist—
	Luke 7:19–29
	The widow's mites—Luke 21:1–4
	A resurrection question—
	Mark 12:18–27
	The Great Commandment—
	Matthew 22:34–40
Wednesday:	The chief priests—Matthew 26:1–5
	The alabaster box—
	Matthew 26:6–13
	Judas's betrayal, three accounts—
	Matthew 26:14–16
	Mark 14:10–11
	John 13:1–2
Thursday:	Preparation for Passover, three
	accounts—
	Matthew 26:17–19
	Mark 14:12–16
	Luke 22:7–13
Friday:	The Disciples—Matthew 26:20–35
	The Garden—Matthew 26:36–56
	Religious trial—
	Matthew 26:57–27:2
	Roman trial—
	Matthew 27:11–31

Peter's denial—
John 18:15–27
Saturday: The Crucifixion, four accounts—
Matthew 27:32–66
Mark 15:15–47
Luke 23:27–56
John 19:23–42
Sunday: The Resurrection, four
accounts—
Matthew 28:1–20
Mark 16:1–18
Luke 24:1–51
John 20:1–29

Other Activities for Families this Week:

• Watch a video on the life of Jesus
• Attend a passion play
• Attend an Easter sunrise service
• Attend an Easter concert
• Read aloud the children's poems and stories included in this book
• Sing selected hymns together at home each day, focusing on selected themes, such as: The Birth of Jesus; Jesus and Me; Worshiping the Lord; The Sacrifice of Praise; Spreading the Good News; The Glory of the Cross; Following Jesus; He Is Risen!

The Lamb

Little Lamb, who made thee?
Dost thou know who made thee?
Gave thee life & bid thee feed
By the stream & o'er the mead;
Gave thee clothing of delight,
Softest clothing wooly bright;
Gave thee such a tender voice,
Making all the vales rejoice:
Little Lamb, who made thee?
Dost thou know who made thee?
Little Lamb, I'll tell thee,
Little Lamb, I'll tell thee:
He is called by thy name,
For he calls himself a Lamb:
He is meek & He is mild,
He became a little child:
I a child & thou a lamb,
We are called by his name.
Little Lamb, God bless thee.
Little Lamb, God bless thee.

—William Blake

Jessie's Easter Bonnet

No point in saying anything to Mother, thought Jessie dismally. *I know if she could, she would probably buy me the frilly, pink-and-white hat in Arenson's display window, but we simply can't afford it.*

Jessie's mom, Alice, was a widow with three children besides Jessie to feed and clothe. But that fact didn't stop the yearning in ten-year-old Jessie's heart. If only once she could have some new clothes like the other kids instead of "make-do's" and "hand-me-downs"! She knew that her best friend Sally had already bought a beautiful blue-and-white dress for Easter. And Sally's grandmother was buying her a hat and shoes to match.

"Jessie, why are you so quiet?" Alice asked her.

"Well. . .I was thinking about the beautiful hat in Arenson's window. . ." Jessie's voice trailed away.

"Oh, Jessie, I'm sorry we can't get it for you. The twins need new shoes."

Later that day as Jessie stood outside Arenson's admiring "her" hat, Mr. Arenson stepped outside. "Something in the window catch your eye?"

Jessie nodded shyly, then hesitatingly, and with a longing that surprised her, she pointed to the beribboned hat. "That hat over there. I think it's the most beautiful one I've ever seen!"

"You're Alice Simpson's little girl, aren't you?"

"Yes, sir," she replied politely.

"Your mother's a mighty fine woman. I know it's been hard on her these past four years since your daddy's been gone. Hmm," said Mr. Arenson, "I need to check on something. Wait right here, would you?"

A few minutes later, he returned carrying a big square box. "Here, this is for you," he said, handing it to her. "But don't open it 'til you get home."

Jessie breathed a whispery, surprised thanks, then carefully walked down the street, anxious to get home and open the box.

"Look, Mom," she called, coming in the back door. "Mr. Arenson gave me this box." Deftly she unwrapped it and looked inside. There, in all of its pink-and-white Easter finery, was a hat exactly like the one in the window!

"Ooooh, Mom, look! It's the hat I wanted! How good of Mr. Arenson to give it to me! I must go back and thank him again at once!"

Although Jessie attended church that Easter Sunday wearing last year's slightly faded dress, no one noticed. They were too busy admiring the beaming face under the lovely pink-and-white hat. That was the happiest Easter Jessie could ever remember.

The Joy of Easter

Excitement glowed on Linda's eager face. "Hurry up, Robert, or we'll be late for the service!"

Robert, still rubbing sleep from his light-blue eyes, cautiously made his way to the living room. It was already 5:15, and the sunrise service, atop a nearby mountain, was scheduled to start at 6:00.

"I finally found my cuff link. Let's go, Linda. We haven't any time to lose."

As the two settled into their old Mercury, a shiver ran down Linda's spine. The cool springtime air rushed past the car. Outside the window, though not yet visible in the early morning shadows, she could picture the blooming yellow daffodils and the budding dogwood trees.

"Oh Robert, isn't it wonderful to know the Lord—and to know He lives inside of us?"

Robert nodded his agreement, adding, "What a difference Jesus has made in our lives! The peace and love and joy He has brought to us is beyond words! Linda, He has transformed our marriage!"

"I know. I'm so glad we know Him." Within a short time, Linda and Robert worshiped the Lord at their first Easter sunrise service. They had come to know Him only three short months earlier, but they knew Jesus was alive—He was alive within their hearts.

Ivan's Easter Service
by Amelia W. Swayne

Ivan was a little Russian boy who lived in the city of St. Petersburg. It was the day before Easter, and he was very happy because he was to be allowed to go to the great church for the midnight service. His sister, Sonia, who was older than he was, had gone the year before and remembered much of what had happened.

As they set out from their home, Ivan asked, "Why is the church so dark when we go in?"

"Because people are remembering the time when everyone thought Jesus was dead," said his mother.

"That was a very dark time," said his father. "People thought the light of the world had gone out. The darkness of the church is to remind us of that time."

Soon they came to the church. As they went in, each one was given a candle. Ivan carried his very carefully and sat down quietly beside his father. He could hear the soft music, but he could not see the great organ. Up on the altar a low light burned. The priest was beginning the service. He sang many parts of it, and the choir replied from time to time. Ivan could not understand all they were saying, but the music was very beautiful, and he was glad to be sitting there close to his father.

The priest finished his prayer and, with the other priests and the choir, walked down the aisle. Ivan could hear the swish of their robes as they passed him. They left the church, and now all was very, very quiet and very, very dark. Ivan sat as still as he could and tried to think how the world would be if no one remembered the things that Jesus had taught.

Suddenly the great bells rang out, and the whole church seemed to become full of light. Easter day had come! The priests and choir marched in singing joyfully, "He is risen," and everyone seemed very happy. A priest held out a shining taper, and Ivan reached up to it to light his candle. He now saw the church was crowded with people all lighting candles. Soon after they had done this, the service ended, and everyone started home carrying his light carefully.

"Christ is risen!" said Ivan's father.

"He is risen indeed!" replied his mother.

"Christ is risen!" said Sonia.

"He is risen indeed!" said Ivan.

Ivan was very happy. He was glad he had gone to the church. He was glad that he could carry home his bright candle.

"It would still be dark if we were not carrying our lights, wouldn't it?" he said.

A KITCHEN ADVENTURE

Easter Cookies
(Sugar shapes)

2 cups sifted cake flour
1½ teaspoons baking powder
½ teaspoon baking soda
3 squares unsweetened
    chocolate, melted
½ teaspoon cinnamon

1 cup sugar
1 egg unbeaten
¼ teaspoon salt
2 tablespoons milk
½ cup margarine

Sift the flour, then measure. Add remaining dry ingredients, and sift 3 times. Cream margarine, adding sugar gradually, until light and fluffy. Add egg and chocolate. Beat well. Add the dry mixture to the wet mixture a small amount at a time, mixing well after each addition. Add milk. Chill thoroughly.

Roll dough to ⅛ inch thickness on a lightly floured board. Cut out in shapes of crosses, angels, etc. Brush with a glaze of 1 egg yolk beaten into ½ cup milk. Bake on an ungreased baking sheet at 350 degrees for 7–9 minutes. Remove from the oven, cool, and outline the edges with a frosting of powdered sugar and egg white squeezed through a cone of paper.

Lamb Aram
(Lamb with Red Noodles)

1½ pounds neck or breast of lamb
¼ teaspoon pepper
1 clove garlic, minced
a dash of cayenne
1 6-ounce can tomato paste
1 5-ounce package broad noodles
3 cups water
1 bay leaf
¼ cup grated cheese
1½ teaspoons salt

Cut the meat into stew-sized pieces. Brown meat slowly in a large heavy skillet without added fat. Add garlic, tomato paste, water, and seasonings. Cover and cook slowly for an hour and 15 minutes. Add the uncooked noodles, making sure that the sauce covers the noodles. (Add more water as the noodles cook, if necessary.) Cover and simmer for 20 minutes, or until the noodles are tender. Before serving, sprinkle with grated cheese.

To enjoy the fresh, springtime flavor of mint with lamb, combine ⅓ cup chopped mint leaves, 2 tablespoons sugar, and ½ cup hot vinegar and stir until sugar dissolves.

Mareshah Cakes
(Cornmeal Cakes)

1 egg, beaten
1¼ cups buttermilk
   (or sour milk)*
¼ cup salad oil
1 tablespoon light molasses
1 cup enriched flour
1 teaspoon salt
2 teaspoons baking powder
½ teaspoon baking soda
½ cup yellow cornmeal

*Milk can be soured by adding 1 tablespoon vinegar to one cup milk.

Combine egg, milk, oil, and molasses. Add sifted dry ingredients and cornmeal. Stir until just barely moistened. Pouring batter from a ¼ cup measure, bake on a hot, ungreased griddle.

   Serve with maple sugar, or as a bread to accompany a chicken dish such as fricassee. A cup of finely chopped ham or a cup of whole-kernel corn added to this batter makes a main dish for a noonday luncheon. Makes 12 cakes.

Haddock Galilee
(Broiled Haddock)

1 pound haddock or other fillets
1 tablespoon melted butter
¾ teaspoon salt
⅛ teaspoon pepper
4 tablespoons butter or margarine
1½ tablespoons lemon juice
a dash of paprika
2 teaspoons minced parsley
2 teaspoons chopped onion
½ teaspoon basil

Arrange the fillets in a buttered or greased shallow, glass baking dish. Brush each fillet with some of the melted butter and sprinkle with salt and pepper. Broil about 2 inches from the heat until lightly browned and flaky. (Never turn fish while broiling.) Meanwhile, cream the 4 tablespoons butter, then blend in the remaining ingredients. When the fish is done, remove it from the broiler, spread it with the herb butter, and place it under the broiler again for a few moments. (Any fish may be cooked in this manner; experiment with other herbs in the butter topping to vary the flavor.)

For a tasty, easy dinner, also serve buttered string beans, mashed potatoes, hot rolls, and a black cherry gelatin whip.

Peppers Capernaum
(Cheese-Stuffed Peppers)

6 green peppers
1½ cups cottage cheese
2½ cups cooked rice
1 egg
salt and pepper to taste
buttered soft crumbs

Wash the peppers. Remove stems, seeds, and white fiber by cutting a circle around each stem. Slice off and chop a half-inch ring from the top of each pepper. Drop peppers into boiling, salted water and cook about five minutes or until barely tender. Drain. Mix the remaining ingredients, except for the bread crumbs. Add the chopped bits of pepper. Fill the peppers with this mixture, top with bread crumbs, and place in a buttered baking dish. Bake at 375 degrees for about 25 minutes. Serves 6.

(Whenever a recipe calls for buttered bread crumbs, save time by topping with dry crumbs, dotting generously with bits of butter, and then baking. Gives the same results.)

Corinth Lentil Soup

1 cup dried lentils
2 cups chopped onion
2 quarts water
1 tablespoon salt
3 tablespoons lemon juice
$1/4$ teaspoon pepper
2 cups chopped raw spinach or Swiss chard
1 tablespoon oil

Soak the lentils overnight. Rinse several times in cold water. Cook lentils, onions, and salt and pepper in 2 quarts of water until the lentils are tender—about $1 1/2$ hours. Add the remaining ingredients and cook 20 minutes longer, or until the spinach or chard is tender. Serves 8.

Shepherd's Shake
(Fruit Milk Shake)

Put 3 tablespoons of any sieved, puréed fruit (canned baby food fruit works well) in a glass. Add $1/2$ teaspoon sugar and a dash of cinnamon. Stir, then fill with chilled milk. Shake or stir vigorously. Garnish with fruit or a sprig of mint.

Scripture Cake
(For Sunday dessert)

4½ cups 1 Kings 4:22 (flour)
1 cup Judges 5:25, last clause (butter)
2 cups Jeremiah 6:20 (sugar)
2 cups 1 Samuel 30:12, second clause (raisins)
2 cups Nahum 3:12 (figs)
2 cups Numbers 17:8 (almonds)
2 tablespoons 1 Samuel 14:25 (honey)
1 pinch Leviticus 2:13 (salt)
6 Jeremiah 17:11 (eggs)
½ cup Judges 4:19, second sentence (milk)
seasonings, 2 Chronicles 9:9 (spices)

Follow the directions of Solomon for bringing up a child, Proverbs 23:14; that is, "beat with a rod." Just as a matter of accuracy, this is a simple butter cake, but with little leavening except the air and eggs; bake it as a loaf at 325 degrees for about 50 minutes. When it tests done, turn out onto a rack until cool. Slices best after a few hours.

TRADITIONS
OF THE
SEASON

Traditions, in and of themselves, are not necessarily something to adhere to—or abandon. Often traditions are the equivalent of "We've always done it this way," and sometimes nobody can even recall why it was done in that particular fashion initially. The Easter season is rich in tradition, and while the events can be enjoyed even while overlooking many traditions, the observance of those traditions, coupled with the understanding of them, can enrich our commemorative experience.

Shrove Tuesday

The tradition actually begins on the last day before the Lenten season, Shrove Tuesday. Traditionally this was the day Christians went to confession and were "shriven," or absolved from their sins. (The word "shrove" is a form of "shriven.") We, however, can come to Jesus directly every day, confess our sins, and receive His forgiveness. We need not wait for "Shrove Tuesday"!

> Search me, O God, and know my heart:
> try me, and know my thoughts:
> And see if there be any wicked way in me,
> and lead me in the way everlasting.
>
> Psalm 139:23–24

> If we confess our sins,
> he is faithful and just to forgive us our sins,
> and to cleanse us from all unrighteousness.
>
> 1 John 1:9

Because Shrove Tuesday was also the last opportunity for merrymaking and indulgence in food and drink before the austere Lenten period, it gained the appellation of "Fat Tuesday." From other customs of making donuts or pancakes on this day, it is also informally called "Donut Day" or "Pancake Day."

The pancake was likely one bread which the

housewife of Jesus' time loved, since it was quick, filling, and economical. She may have baked hers on a hot stone; some housewives, no doubt, used a hole dug in the ground for their oven. In this, the sides were smoothly plastered and the fire was placed in the bottom. When it was sufficiently heated, the bread or cake was placed on the smooth sides and baked swiftly.

Try making the mareshah cakes (cornmeal cakes) suggested in the Kitchen Adventure!

The Season of Lent

From before the foundations of the world, Jesus was preparing for what would happen in the last few days of his life. That we prepare ourselves for the remembrance of this significant season is only fitting. The days during which we give particular attention to preparation for Easter—a forty-day period beginning with Ash Wednesday and extending, with the omission of Sundays, to the day before Easter—is called the Lenten season. Of the Sundays of Lent, the first is Passion Sunday, and the last is Palm Sunday. The week preceding Easter, including Good Friday, is Holy Week. Lent ends at midnight on the Saturday before Easter Sunday.

Observed as a time of penitence, abstinence, and fasting, Lent began early in church history to commemorate Christ's forty-day fast in the wilderness. The word "Lent" simply means "springtime," and has varying traditions associated with it.

The early Christians used the Lenten season as a time for instruction of new converts which culminated in their pre-Easter baptism. Thus it was both a time of learning about the Christian faith as well as a time of moral examination and soul-searching.

This time of self-examination can take place between a Christian and the Lord and consists of humbling oneself before Him, of praying, and of various kinds of fasting. The apostle Paul admonishes us to "Examine yourselves, whether ye be in the faith" (2 Corinthians 13:5).

Ash Wednesday

Lent commences with Ash Wednesday, so named from the ceremonial use of ashes as a symbol of penitence. The custom in some churches is for the priest, after prayer, to take ashes and make the sign of the Cross on a believer's forehead.

Although many Protestant churches do not practice this custom, the accompanying command can nevertheless be taken to heart:

"Remember, man, that thou art dust and
unto dust thou shalt return."

Fasting

Because the general concept of fasting is too vast a subject to cover here, only fasting as it relates to Lent will be discussed. Fasting could be defined broadly as "self-denial." The range of interpretation varies: denying one's self food, whether skipping a meal (or several meals) or choosing not to eat a favorite food, can be considered fasting. Of course, the gamut of reasons for fasting reaches from humbling one's self to bringing more discipline into one's life. Although in general fasting, the participants can be an individual or a nation, Lenten fasting is focused on the individual to engender personal spiritual introspection and a closer relationship with God.

> Precious Savior, why do I fear Your scrutiny? Yours is an examen of love. Still, I am afraid. . .afraid of what may surface. Even so, I invite You to search me to the depths so that I may know myself—and You—in fuller measure. Amen.
>
> —Richard J. Foster

The most important aspect of fasting is the heart motive. Once this spiritual discipline is chosen, it needs to be practiced as unto the Lord. The classic scriptural passage concerning fasting is found in Isaiah 58. Early in this chapter, God says to His people: "Behold, in the day of your fast ye find pleasure." Then He describes the fast that He delights in:

Is not this the fast that I have chosen?
to loose the bands of wickedness, to
undo the heavy burdens, and to let the
oppressed go free, and that ye break
every yoke?
Is it not to deal thy bread to the hungry,
and that thou bring the poor that are cast
out to thy house? when thou seest the
naked, that thou cover him; and that
thou hide not thyself from thine own flesh?
Then shall thy light break forth as the morning,
and thine health shall spring forth speedily:
and thy righteousness shall go before thee; the
glory of the LORD shall be thy rereward.
Then shalt thou call, and the LORD shall
answer; thou shalt cry, and he shall say,
Here I am.

Isaiah 58:6–9

John Wesley and the early Methodists disciplined themselves to fast every Friday. While the timing does not relate to Lent, some of Wesley's insight on the subject of fasting, summarized in the well-known Sermon 27, is beneficial:

First, let it be done unto the Lord, with our eye

singly fixed on Him. Let our intention herein be this, and this alone, to glorify our Father which is in heaven; to express our sorrow and shame for our manifold transgressions of His holy law; to wait for an increase of purifying grace, drawing our affections to things above; to add seriousness and earnestness to our prayers; to avert the wrath of God; and to obtain all the great and precious promises which He hath made to us in Jesus Christ. . . . Fasting is only a way which God hath ordained, wherein we wait for His unmerited mercy; and wherein, without any desert of ours, He hath promised freely to give us His blessing.

Palm Sunday

The crowds widely acclaimed Jesus as He rode into Jerusalem on a donkey. . .they spread palm branches in His path and cried:

"Hosanna to the Son of David!" "Blessed is he who comes in the name of the Lord!" "Hosanna in the highest!" (Matthew 21:9, NIV).

The Palms

O'er all the way green palms and blossoms
gay—
Are strewn this day, in festal preparation.
Where Jesus comes to wipe our tears away—
E'en now the throng to welcome Him prepare;

CHORUS
Join all and sing His name declare,
Hosanna! Praise to the Lord!
Bless Him who cometh to bring us salvation!

His word goes forth and people by its might—
Once more regain freedom from degradation.
Humanity doth give to each his right—
While those in darkness are restored to light.

Sing and rejoice, O blest Jerusalem,
Of all thy sons sing the emancipation,
Through boundless love the Christ of
Bethlehem—
Brings faith and hope to thee forevermore.
—J. Faure

Maundy Thursday

Following Jesus' triumphal entry into the city of Jerusalem on Palm Sunday, He continued to teach, preach, and heal. His disciples prepared the Passover meal, as He directed, for Thursday evening. This Thursday is known as Maundy Thursday, the name "Maundy" being derived from the first word in an anthem traditionally sung in a ceremony on that day. In England, a custom survives of giving "maundy pennies" (or alms) to the poor, recalling an earlier practice in which the sovereign washed the feet of the poor on Maundy Thursday. In most European countries, the day is simply known as Holy Thursday.

During Thursday evening, Jesus washed His disciples' feet, broke the bread, and poured out the wine.

ACCORDING TO THY GRACIOUS WORD

According to Thy gracious Word,
In meek humility,
This will I do, my dying Lord,
I will remember Thee.

Thy body, broken for my sake,
My bread from heav'n shall be;
Thy testamental cup I take,

And thus remember Thee.

Gethsemane, can I forget?
Or there Thy conflict see,
Thine agony and bloody sweat,
And not remember Thee?

When to the cross I turn mine eyes,
And rest on Calvary,
Lamb of God, my Sacrifice,
I must remember Thee.
　　　　　　　　—James Montgomery

After the Passover meal, He shared His heart and soul with His followers before offering a prayer for them as recorded in John chapters thirteen to seventeen.

"And now, Father, glorify me in your presence with the glory I had with you before the world began. I have revealed you to those whom you gave me out of the world. . . . For I gave them the words you gave me and they accepted them. They knew with certainty that I came from you, and they believed that you sent me. . . . My prayer is not that you take them out of the world but that you protect them from the evil one. . . . My prayer is not for them alone. I pray also for those who will believe in me through their message" (John 17:5–6, 8, 15, 20, NIV).

In commemoration, the Last Supper, known also as Communion, is commonly served, and the ceremony of the washing of the feet is performed. Participants sometimes wash the feet of twelve people, symbolic of Christ's washing of His disciples' feet.

Following the Passover meal, Jesus went to the Garden of Gethsemane where He prayed, "O my Father, if it be possible, let this cup pass from me: nevertheless not as I will, but as thou wilt" (Matthew 26:39).

Momentarily, Judas arrived with a band of soldiers and kissed Jesus on the cheek—a predetermined gesture of betrayal, and the Roman soldiers took Jesus into custody. During the next several hours, Jesus was tried by a religious court and then by civil courts under Pontius Pilate and King Herod. Pilate expressed reluctance to sentence Jesus because he believed in His innocence, but succumbed when the Jerusalem mob cried, "Crucify Him, crucify Him!"

Good Friday

Jesus was crucified on Friday, the day after Passover. The Jewish priests convicted Him on the charge that He had blasphemed God. As a matter of course, two thieves were also put to death on crosses the same day, one on each side of Jesus.

The Date of Easter

The dates for Easter (the Resurrection of Christ) and the Jewish Passover coincided in the first century: since Judaism's calendar was based on the lunar cycle, both events followed the first full moon in the spring. Much conflict resulted from both celebrations being held at the same time. The Christians wanted to begin a week-long celebration of Christ's Resurrection, and they wished to have it begin on Sunday, but Passover does not fall on any particular weekday.

Constantine the Great summoned the famous Council of Nicaea in A.D. 325 to resolve the date of Easter—and all the anxiety the churches had over it! It was decided that Easter must be celebrated everywhere on the same day and that this day must be a Sunday. It was further decided that to avoid any coincidental celebration, it must be the first Sunday after the full moon following the vernal equinox,

March 21, with one reservation. The English prayer book states: "If the full moon happens upon a Sunday, Easter-day is the Sunday after."

New Clothes

The custom of new clothes for Easter began when the early Christian converts were baptized the day before Easter. After their baptism, they put on new clothing to show their new life in Christ!

New clothes are exciting and they give us an emotional lift, but we should always remember how this tradition began and celebrate our inner life in Christ more than our outward display of new clothes!

EASTER
MEDITATIONS

The specific purpose of our preparation is the benefit and blessing that can be ours through contemplation of the events surrounding the days preceding and including Easter. As we now ponder the significance of His humility in becoming human, His submission to the will of His Father, His suffering for our sin, and His redemption of mankind, may the love in our hearts erupt into expressions of praise and adoration to Him.

Jesus was chosen before the foundations of the world to come to earth as a tiny baby born in Bethlehem. He who is "Wonderful, Counsellor, The mighty God, The everlasting Father, The Prince of Peace" (Isaiah 9:6) willingly came not only in the form of a man but as a totally helpless infant.

Then, not only as an infant, but to the poorest of the poor, in the lowest of the lowliest. "And she [Mary] brought forth her firstborn son, and wrapped him in swaddling clothes, and laid him in a manger; because there was no room for them in the inn" (Luke 2:7).

Ivory Palaces

My Lord has garments so wondrous fine,
And myrrh their texture fills;
Its fragrance reached to this heart of mine,
With joy my being thrills.

His life had also its sorrows sore,
For aloes had a part;
And when I think of the cross He bore,
My eyes with teardrops start.

CHORUS
Out of the ivory palaces
Into a world of woe,
Only His great eternal love
Made my Savior go.

—Henry Barraclough

Hail the blest morn! when the great Mediator
Down from the regions of glory descends!

—Reginald Heber

In the beginning was the Word,
and the Word was with God,
and the Word was God. . . .
And the Word was made flesh,
and dwelt among us. . . .

John 1:1, 14

Jesus "dwelt among us," living life at our level, walking with us by the way, visiting in our homes, eating at our tables, blessing our children. Emmanuel: God with us.

He calmed the storm.

Then he arose, and rebuked the winds and the sea; and there was a great calm. But the men marvelled, saying, What manner of man is this, that even the winds and the sea obey him! (Matthew 8:26–27).

He fed the multitudes.

And Jesus saith unto them, How many loaves have ye? And they said, Seven, and a few little fishes. And he commanded the multitude to sit down on the ground. And he took the seven loaves and the fishes, and gave thanks, and brake them, and gave to. . . the multitude. . . . And they that did eat were four thousand men, beside women and children (Matthew 15:34–36, 38).

He cast out evil spirits.

For he said unto him, Come out of the man, thou unclean spirit. And he asked him, What is thy name? And he answered, My name is Legion: for we are many. . . . And all the devils besought him, saying, Send us into the swine. . . . And forthwith Jesus gave them leave. And the unclean spirits went out. . . . (Mark 5:8–9, 12–13).

He healed the sick.

And great multitudes came unto him, having with them those that were lame, blind, dumb, maimed, and many others, and cast them down at Jesus' feet; and he healed them: Insomuch that the multitude wondered, when they saw the dumb to speak, the maimed to be whole, the lame to walk, and the blind to see: and they glorified the God of Israel (Matthew 15:30–31).

He ministered to the needy.

Jesus answered and said unto them. . .The blind receive their sight, and the lame walk, the lepers are cleansed, and the deaf hear, the dead are raised up, and the poor have the gospel preached to them (Matthew 11:4–5).

They Seldom Show Him with a Smile

They seldom show Him with a smile.
    Always His face is sad to see,
    As if a jest could never be
Nor He be merry for a while.
The kindly humor that could pat
    The brows of boys He chanced to see
    And say: "Let children come to me!"
No brush has ever pictured that!

The man who loved a little child
    And walked the common ways of men,
    Though troubled often, now and then
With those about Him surely smiled.
I fancy as I read His word
    I hear Him chuckling, soft and sweet,
    Telling to Mary, at His feet,
Some curious thing He'd seen or heard.

He must have had a twinkling eye,
    Which danced at times with gentle mirth,
    So greatly to be loved on earth,
So bravely on the cross to die.

—Edgar A. Guest

Fairest Lord Jesus

Fairest Lord Jesus!
Ruler of all nature!
O Thou of God and man the Son!
Thee will I cherish,
Thee will I honor,
Thou my soul's glory, joy, and crown!

. . . .

Fair is the sunshine,
Fairer still the moonlight,
And all the twinkling starry host;
Jesus shines brighter,
Jesus shines purer
Than all the angels heav'n can boast!

Beautiful Savior!
Lord of all the Nations!
Son of God and Son of Man!
Glory and honor,
Praise, adoration
Now and forevermore be Thine!

Who, being in very nature God, did not consider
equality with God something to be grasped, but
made himself nothing, taking the very nature of
a servant, being made in human likeness. And
being found in appearance as a man, he humbled
himself and became obedient to death—even
death on a cross!

Philippians 2:6–8, NIV

Jesus counted the cost of coming to this world,
knowing that He "came not to be ministered unto,
but to minister, and to give his life a ransom for
many" (Matthew 20:28). Still, He deliberately came
to give "himself for us an offering and a sacrifice to
God for a sweetsmelling savour" (Ephesians 5:2), and
did not swerve from His purpose. He set His face like
a flint to do His Father's will. Following His baptism
in the River Jordan by John the Baptist, Jesus was led
by the Holy Spirit into the wilderness for forty days
where He prayed and fasted. Afterward, He endured
Satan's temptations, which centered around: 1)
Food, 2) Power, and 3) Wealth and Fame. To each of
these temptations, Jesus responded with Scripture.

In response to the temptation, "command that
these stones be made bread," Jesus told Satan: "Man
shall not live by bread alone, but by every word that
proceedeth out of the mouth of God." Next, the devil
challenged, "If thou be the Son of God, cast thyself
down: for it is written, He shall give his angels charge
concerning thee: and in their hands they shall bear
thee up, lest at any time thou dash thy foot against a

stone." Jesus told him, "It is written again, Thou shalt not tempt the Lord thy God." To the last temptation, when the devil set Jesus on a high mountain and showed Him the kingdoms of the world, offering to give them to Him in return for His worship, Jesus responded, "Get thee hence, Satan: for it is written, Thou shalt worship the Lord thy God, and him only shalt thou serve" (Matthew 4:1–10).

Almost immediately, Jesus began to preach saying, "Repent: for the kingdom of heaven is at hand" (Matthew 4:17). As He walked near the Sea of Galilee, Jesus saw two fishermen, Peter and Andrew. He called them to become His disciples and follow Him. Ultimately, Jesus gathered twelve disciples, calling them to leave everything and follow Him. "And he said to them all, If any man will come after me, let him deny himself, and take up his cross daily, and follow me" (Luke 9:23).

What He asked of His disciples was no less than what He Himself was doing. He continually was denying Himself and carrying His cross. No one diverted his attention from His mission. "When the time was come that he should be received up, he stedfastly set his face to go to Jerusalem" (Luke 9:51).

He was despised and rejected by men, a man of sorrows, and familiar with suffering. . . . Surely he took up our infirmities and carried our sorrows, yet we considered him stricken by God, smitten by him, and afflicted. But he was pierced for our transgressions, he was crushed

for our iniquities; the punishment that brought
us peace was upon him, and by his wounds we
are healed (Isaiah 53:3–5, NIV).

Continuing this time of meditation, let's reflect on
the death Jesus endured for us on the cross.
Salvation is free to us, but it was not free to Jesus
Christ. He suffered unspeakable torture and agony
as He paid the penalty of our sins and opened the
way for us to enter heaven. Charles Spurgeon had
the following thoughts concerning the meaning of
the cross:

> In the cross of Christ we glory, because
> we regard it as a matchless exhibition of
> the attributes of God. . . . In the cross we
> see a strange conjunction of what once
> appeared to be two opposite qualities—
> justice and mercy. . . . We can never tell
> which of the attributes of God shines
> most glorious in the sacrifice of Christ;
> they each one find a glorious high throne
> in the person and work of the Lamb of
> God, that taketh away the sin of the
> world. Since it has become, as it were,
> the disc which reflects the character
> and perfections of God, it is meet that
> we should glory in the cross of Christ,
> and none shall stay us of our boasting.

But God forbid that I should glory, save in the cross of our Lord Jesus Christ, by whom the world is crucified unto me, and I unto the world (Galatians 6:14).

When I Survey the Wondrous Cross

When I survey the wondrous cross,
On which the Prince of glory died,
My richest gain I count but loss,
And pour contempt on all my pride.

Forbid it, Lord, that I should boast,
Save in the death of Christ, my God;
All the vain things that charm me most,
I sacrifice them to His blood.
. . . .
Were the whole realm of nature mine,
That were a present far too small;
Love so amazing, so divine,
Demands my soul, my life, my all.
—Isaac Watts

Granted, the cross is a gruesome instrument of igno-
minious death, but we see glory shining through it
because of its effect upon our lives. Jesus has invited
whosoever will to come and experience the life-
changing, purifying impact of His finished work
upon the cross. Whosoever will. Think on it!
Regardless of our status in life, our past, our char-
acteristics, or our abilities, the requirement of redemption has been fully satisfied. Nothing remains for us to
do but to accept for ourselves the forgiveness of our
sins. Only our own refusal to come can exclude us
from the blessings of His grace.

A Prayer of Petition

Almighty and everlasting God, who hatest
nothing that Thou hast made, and dost for-
give the sins of all those who are penitent;
Create and make in us new and contrite
hearts, that we, worthily lamenting our sins
and acknowledging our wretchedness, may
obtain of Thee, the God of all mercy, perfect remission and forgiveness; through
Jesus Christ our Lord. Amen.
                        —Book of Common Prayer

Through Jesus, therefore, let us continually offer to God a sacrifice of praise—the fruit of lips that confess his name (Hebrews 13:15, NIV).

You are Lord

Lord, I delight myself in You!
Out of the joy welling from my depths
I bless Your name.
I kneel before You in worship,
singing alleluia.
Let my praises be my sacrifice to You,
the outpouring of my life,
the offering of my faith.
Jesus, You are Lord!
I confess Your name, Your salvation.
I praise You for being my Lord!
                              —Lois Walfrid Johnson
                         Songs for Silent Moments

Heavenly Father, thank You for so loving the world, that You gave Your only begotten Son, that I might believe in Him and not perish, but have everlasting life.

Amen.

I Praise You

It seemed impossible,
but You did it again!
For moments of sunlight
That are beams of grace
in my life or the lives of others,
I praise You, Spirit of God!
For miracles I pray for
And yet forget to expect,
I praise You!

For the joy of a new Christian,
For evidence that You have worked
in that life, I praise You!
For Your glow in a believer,
For Your continuing growth,
I praise You!
I rejoice in Your light;
I praise You!

—Lois Walfrid Johnson
Songs for Silent Moments

I Believe In Miracles

Creation shows the power of God—
There's glory all around,
And those who see must stand in awe
For miracles abound.
I cannot doubt the work of God,
It's plain for all to see;
The miracles that He has wrought
Should lead to Calvary.
The love of God! O power divine!
'Tis wonderful to see
The miracle of grace performed
Within the heart of me.
I believe in miracles
I've seen a soul set free,
Miraculous the change in one
redeemed through Calvary;
I've seen the lily push its way
up through the stubborn sod—
I believe in miracles
For I believe in God!

—Carlton C. Buck

O For A Thousand Tongues to Sing

O for a thousand tongues to sing
My great Redeemer's praise,
The glories of my God and King,
The triumphs of His grace.

. . . .

Jesus! the name that charms our fears,
That bids our sorrows cease;
'Tis music in the sinner's ears,
'Tis life, and health, and peace.

He breaks the pow'r of canceled sin,
He sets the pris'ner free;
His blood can make the foulest clean;
His blood availed for me.

Hear Him, ye deaf; His praise, ye dumb,
Your loosened tongues employ;
Ye blind, behold your Savior come;
And leap, ye lame, for joy.
—Charles Wesley

A Prayer
for the Transforming
of Everyday Life

Father, in these quiet moments we have caught a glimpse of Thy glory. Inspire us, our Father, to carry into the everydayness of our lives all to which we aspire at such a moment as this. May our faith have feet and hands, a voice and a heart, that it may minister to others, that the gospel we profess may shine in our faces and be seen in our lives.

May we return to face the grind of the monotonous and the humdrum routine of duty with a new vision. Wilt Thou transform for us our common tasks and glorify them with a new light, that we may this week apply ourselves to them with fidelity and devotion. . . .

May Thy blessing rest upon all men who minister to their fellows. May each of us in our daily round come to know the joy of partnership with Thee, our Father in Heaven. In the name of Him who came "not to be ministered unto but to minister," we join these, our prayers. Amen.

—Peter Marshall

SPURGEON'S
PASSION
WEEK
DEVOTIONALS

Monday Morning

"Jesus answered If. . .therefore ye seek me, let these go their way." JOHN 18:8

Mark, my soul, the care which Jesus manifested even in His hour of trial, towards the sheep of His hand! The ruling passion is strong in death. He resigns himself to the enemy, but He interposes a word of power to set His disciples free. As to Himself, like a sheep before her shearers He is dumb and opened not His mouth, but for His disciples' sake He speaks with Almighty energy. Herein is love, constant, self-forgetting, faithful love. But is there not far more here than is to be found upon the surface? Have we not the very soul and spirit of the atonement in these words? The Good Shepherd lays down His life for the sheep, and pleads that they must therefore go free. The Surety is bound, and justice demands that those for whom He stands a substitute should go their way. In the midst of Egypt's bondage, that voice rings as a word of power, *"Let these go their way."* Out of slavery of sin and Satan the redeemed must come. In every cell of the dungeons of Despair, the sound is echoed, *"Let these go their way,"* and forth come Despondency and Much-afraid. Satan hears the well-known voice, and lifts his foot from the neck of the fallen; and Death hears it, and the grave opens her gates to let the dead arise. *Their way* is one of progress, holiness, triumph, glory, and none shall dare to stay them in it. No lion shall be on their way, neither shall any ravenous beast go up thereon. "The hind of the morning" has drawn the cruel hunters upon Himself, and now the most timid roes and hinds of the field may graze at perfect peace among the lilies of His loves. The thunder-cloud has burst over the Cross of Calvary, and the pilgrims of Zion shall never be smitten by the bolts of vengeance. Come, my heart, rejoice in the immunity which thy Redeemer has secured thee, and bless His name all the day, and every day.

Monday Evening

"Then all the disciples forsook him and fled."
MATTHEW 26:56

He never deserted them, but they in cowardly fear of their lives, fled from Him in the very beginning of His sufferings. This is but one instructive instance of the frailty of all believers if left to themselves; they are but sheep at the best, and they flee when the wolf cometh. They had all been warned of the danger, and had promised to die rather than leave their Master; and yet they were seized with sudden panic, and took to their heels. It may be, that

I, at the opening of this day, have braced up my mind to bear a trial for the Lord's sake, and I imagine myself to be certain to exhibit perfect fidelity; but let me be very jealous of myself, lest having the same evil heart of unbelief, I should depart from my Lord as the apostles did. It is one thing to promise, and quite another to perform. It would have been to their eternal honour to have stood at Jesus' side right manfully; they fled from honour; may I be kept from imitating them! Where else could they have been so safe as near their Master, who could presently call for twelve legions of angels? They fled from their true safety. O God, let me not play the fool also. Divine grace can make the coward brave. The smoking flax can flame forth like fire on the altar when the Lord wills it. These very apostles who were timid as hares, grew to be bold as lions after the Spirit had descended upon them, and even so the Holy Spirit can make my recreant spirit brave to confess my Lord and witness for His truth.

What anguish must have filled the Saviour as He saw His friends so faithless! This was one bitter ingredient in His cup; but that cup is drained dry; let me not put another drop in it. If I forsake my Lord, I shall crucify Him afresh, and put Him to an open shame. Keep me, O blessed Spirit, from an end so shameful.

Tuesday Morning

"I will accept you with your sweet savour."
EZEKIEL 20:41

The merits of our great Redeemer are as sweet savour to the Most High. Whether we speak of the active or passive righteousness of Christ, there is an equal fragrance. There was a sweet savour in His active life by which He honoured the law of God, and made every precept to glitter like a precious jewel in the pure setting of His own person. Such, too, was His passive obedience, when He endured with unmurmuring submission, hunger and thirst, cold and nakedness, and at length sweat great drops of blood in Gethsemane, gave His back to the smiters, and His cheeks to them that plucked out the hair, and was fastened to the cruel wood, that He might suffer the wrath of God in our behalf. These two things are sweet before the Most High; and for the sake of His doing and His dying, His substitutionary sufferings and His vicarious obedience, the Lord our God accepts us. What a preciousness must there be in Him to overcome our want of preciousness! What a sweet savour to put away our ill savour! What a cleansing power in His blood to take away sin such as ours! and what glory in His righteousness to make such unacceptable creatures to be accepted in the

Beloved! Mark, believer, how sure and unchanging must be our acceptance, since it is *in Him!* Take care that you never doubt your acceptance in Jesus. You cannot be accepted without Christ; but, when you have received His merit, you cannot be unaccepted. Notwithstanding all your doubts, and fears, and sins, Jehovah's gracious eye never looks upon you in anger; though He sees sin in you, in yourself, yet when He looks at you through Christ, He sees no sin. You are always accepted in Christ, are always blessed and dear to the Father's heart. Therefore lift up a song, and as you see the smoking incense of the merit of the Saviour coming up, this evening, before the sapphire throne, let the incense of your praise go up also.

Tuesday Evening

"Though he were a Son, yet learned he obedience by the things which he suffered."

HEBREWS 5:8

We are told that the Captain of our salvation was made perfect through suffering, therefore we who are sinful, and who are far from being perfect, must not wonder if we are called to pass through suffering too. Shall the head be crowned with thorns, and shall the other members of the body be rocked upon the dainty lap of ease? Must Christ pass through seas of his own blood to win the crown, and are we to walk to heaven dryshod in silver slippers? No, our Master's experience teaches us that suffering is necessary, and the true-born child of God must not, would not, escape it if he might. But there is one very comforting thought in the fact of Christ's "being made perfect through suffering"—it is, that He can have complete sympathy with us. "He is not an high priest that cannot be touched with the feeling of our infirmities." In this sympathy of Christ we find a sustaining power. One of the early martyrs said, "I can bear it all, for Jesus suffered, and He suffers in me now; He sympathizes with me, and this makes me strong." Believer, lay hold of this thought in all times of agony. Let the thought of Jesus strengthen you as you follow in His steps. Find a sweet support in His sympathy; and remember that, to suffer is an honourable thing—to suffer for Christ is glory. The apostles rejoiced that they were counted worthy to do this. Just so far as the Lord shall give us grace to suffer *for* Christ, to suffer *with* Christ, just so far does He honour us. The jewels of a Christian are his afflictions. The regalia of the kings whom God hath anointed are their troubles, their sorrows, and their griefs. Let us not, therefore, shun being honoured. Let us not turn aside from being exalted. Griefs exalt us, and troubles lift us up. "If we suffer, we shall also reign with Him."

Wednesday Morning

"He was numbered with the transgressors."

ISAIAH 53:12

Why did Jesus suffer Himself to be enrolled amongst sinners? This wonderful condescension was justified by many powerful reasons. *In such a character He could the better become their advocate.* In some trials there is an identification of the counsellor with the client, nor can they be looked upon in the eye of the law as apart from one another. Now, when the sinner is brought to the bar, Jesus appears there Himself. *He* stands to answer the accusation. He points to His side, His hands, His feet, and challenges Justice to bring anything against the sinners whom He represents; He pleads His blood, and pleads so triumphantly, being numbered with them and having a part with them, that the Judge proclaims, "Let them go their way; deliver them from going down into the pit, for He hath found a ransom." Our Lord Jesus was numbered with the transgressors in order that they might *feel their hearts drawn towards Him.* Who can be afraid of one who is written in the same list with us? Surely we may come boldly to Him, and confess our guilt. He who is numbered with us cannot condemn us. Was He not put down in the transgressor's list *that we might be written in the red roll of the saints?* He was holy, and written among the holy;

we were guilty, and numbered among the guilty; He transfers His name from yonder list to this black indictment, and our names are taken from the indictment and written in the roll of acceptance, for there is a complete transfer made between Jesus and His people. All our estate of misery and sin Jesus has taken; and all that Jesus has comes to us. His righteousness, His blood, and everything that He hath He gives us as our dowry. Rejoice, believer, in your union to Him who was numbered among the transgressors; and prove that you are truly saved by being manifestly numbered with those who are new creatures in Him.

Wednesday Evening

"With his stripes we are healed."

ISAIAH 53:5

Pilate delivered our Lord to the lictors to be scourged. The Roman scourge was a most dreadful instrument of torture. It was made of the sinews of oxen, and sharp bones were intertwisted every here and there among the sinews; so that every time the lash came down these pieces of bone inflicted fearful laceration, and tore off the flesh from the bone. The Saviour was, no doubt, bound to the column, and thus beaten. He had been beaten before; but this of the Roman lictors was probably the most severe of His flagellations. My soul, stand here and weep over His poor stricken body.

Believer in Jesus, can you gaze upon Him without tears, as He stands before you the mirror of agonizing love? He is at once fair as the lily for innocence, and red as the rose with the crimson of His own blood. As we feel the sure and blessed healing which His stripes have wrought in us, does not our heart melt at once with love and grief? If ever we have loved our Lord Jesus, surely we must feel that affection glowing now within our bosoms.

> *"See how the patient Jesus stands,*
> *Insulted in His lowest case!*
> *Sinners have bound the Almighty's hands,*
> *And spit in their Creator's face.*
>
> *With thorns His temples gor'd and gash'd*
> *Send streams of blood from every part;*
> *His back's with knotted scourges lash'd.*
> *But sharper scourges tear His heart."*

We would fain go to our chambers and weep; but since our business calls us away, we will first pray our Beloved to print the image of His bleeding self upon the tablets of our hearts all the day, and at nightfall we will return to commune with Him, and sorrow that our sin should have cost Him so dear.

Thursday Morning

"He answered him to never a word."

MATTHEW 27:14

He had never been slow of speech when He could bless the sons of men, but He would not say a single word for Himself. "Never man spake like this man," and never man was silent like Him. Was this singular silence *the index of His perfect self-sacrifice?* Did it show that He would not utter a word to stay the slaughter of His sacred person, which He had dedicated as an offering for us? Had He so entirely surrendered himself that He would not interfere in His own behalf, even in the minutest degree, but be bound and slain an unstruggling, uncomplaining victim? Was this silence a *type of the defencelessness of sin?* Nothing can be said in palliation or excuse of human guilt; and, therefore, He who bore its whole weight stood speechless before His judge. Is not patient silence *the best reply to a gainsaying world?* Calm endurance answers some questions infinitely more conclusively than the loftiest eloquence. The best apologists for Christianity in the early days were its martyrs. The anvil breaks a host of hammers by quietly bearing their blows. Did not the silent Lamb of God furnish us with *a grand example of wisdom?* Where every word was occasion for new blasphemy, it was the line of duty to afford no fuel for the flame of sin. The ambiguous and the false, the unworthy and mean, will ere long overthrow and confute themselves, and therefore the true can afford to be quiet, and finds silence to be its wisdom. Evidently our Lord, by His silence, furnished *a remarkable fulfillment of prophecy.* A long defence of Himself would have been contrary to Isaiah's prediction. "He is led as a lamb to the slaughter, and as a sheep before her shearers is dumb, so he openeth not his mouth." By His quiet He conclusively proved Himself to be the true Lamb of God. As such we salute Him this morning. Be with us, Jesus, and in the silence of our heart, let us hear the voice of Thy love.

Thursday Evening

"They took Jesus, and led him away."

JOHN 19:16

He had been all night in agony, He had spent the early morning at the hall of Caiaphas, He had been hurried from Caiaphas to Pilate, from Pilate to Herod, and from Herod back again to Pilate; He had, therefore, but little strength left, and yet neither refreshment nor rest were permitted Him. They were eager for His blood, and therefore led Him out to die, loaded with the cross. O dolorous procession! Well may

Salem's daughters weep. My soul, do thou weep also.

What learn we here as we see our blessed Lord led forth? Do we not perceive that truth which was set forth in shadow by *the scapegoat?* Did not the high-priest bring the scapegoat, and put both his hands upon its head, confessing the sins of the people, that thus those sins might be laid upon the goat, and cease from the people? Then the goat was led away by a fit man into the wilderness, and it carried away the sins of the people, so that if they were sought for they could not be found. Now we see Jesus brought before the priests and rulers, who pronounce Him guilty; God Himself imputes our sins *to Him,* "the Lord hath laid on Him the iniquity of us all"; "He was made sin for us"; and, as the substitute for our guilt, bearing our sin upon His shoulders, represented by the cross; we see the great Scapegoat led away by the appointed officers of justice. Beloved, can you feel assured that He carried *your* sin? As you look at the cross upon His shoulders, does it represent *your* sin? There is one way by which you can tell whether He carried your sin or not. Have you laid your hand upon His head, con-fessed your sin, and trusted in Him? Then your sin lies not on you; it has all been transferred by blessed impu-tation to Christ, and He bears it on His shoulder as a load heavier than the cross.

Let not the picture vanish till you have rejoiced in your own deliverance, and adored the loving Redeemer upon whom your iniquities were laid.

Friday Morning

"All we like sheep have gone astray; we have turned every one to his own way; and the LORD hath laid on him the iniquity of us all."

ISAIAH 53:6

Here a confession of sin *common* to all the elect people of God. They have all fallen, and therefore, in common chorus, they all say, from the first who entered heaven to the last who shall enter there, "All we like sheep have gone astray." The confession, while thus unanimous, is also *special* and particular: "We have turned every one to his own way." There is a peculiar sinfulness about every one of the individuals; all are sinful, but each one with some special aggravation not found in his fellow. It is the mark of genuine repentance that while it naturally associates itself with other penitents, it also takes up a position of loneliness. "We have turned every one to his own way," is a confession that each man had sinned against light peculiar to himself, or sinned with an aggravation which he could not perceive in others. This confession is *unreserved*; there is not a word to detract from its force, nor a syllable by way of excuse. The confession is *a giving up of all pleas of self-righteousness.* It is the declaration of men who are consciously guilty—guilty with aggravations, guilty without excuse: they stand with their weapons of rebellion broken in pieces, and cry, "All we like sheep have gone astray; we have turned every one to his own way." Yet we hear no dolorous wailings attending this confession of sin; for the next sentence makes it almost a song. "The Lord hath laid on him the iniquity of us all." It is the most grievous sentence of the three, but it overflows with comfort. Strange is it that where misery was concentrated mercy reigned; where sorrow reached her climax weary souls find rest. The Saviour bruised is the healing of bruised hearts. See how the lowliest penitence gives place to assured confidence through simply gazing at Christ on the cross!

Friday Evening

"On him they laid the cross, that he might bear it after Jesus." LUKE 23:26

We see in Simon's carrying the cross a picture of the work of the Church throughout all generations; she is the cross-bearer after Jesus. Mark then, Christian, Jesus does not suffer so as to exclude your suffering. He bears a cross, not that you may escape it, but that you may endure it. Christ exempts you from sin, but not from sorrow. Remember that, and expect to suffer.

But let us comfort ourselves with this thought, that in our case, as in Simon's, *it is not our cross, but Christ's cross which we carry.* When you are molested for your piety; when your religion brings the trial of cruel mockings upon you, then remember it is not *your* cross, it is *Christ's* cross; and how delightful is it to carry the cross of our Lord Jesus!

You carry the cross after Him. You have blessed company; your path is marked with the footprints of your Lord. The mark of His blood-red shoulder is upon that heavy burden. 'Tis *His* cross, and He goes before you as a shepherd goes before his sheep. Take up your cross daily, and follow Him.

Do not forget, also, *that you bear this cross in partnership.* It is the opinion of some that Simon only carried one end of the cross, and not the whole of it. That is very possible; Christ may have carried the heavier part, against the transverse beam, and Simon may have borne the lighter end. Certainly it is so with you; you do but carry the light end of the cross, Christ bore the heavier end.

And remember, *though Simon had to bear the cross for a very little while, it gave him lasting honour.* Even so the cross *we* carry is only for a little while at most, and then we shall receive the crown, the glory. Surely we should love the cross, and, instead of shrinking from it, *count it very dear,* when it works out for us "a far more exceeding and eternal weight of glory."

Saturday Morning

"And there followed him a great company of people, and of women, which also bewailed and lamented him."

LUKE 23:27

Amid the rabble rout which hounded the Redeemer to His doom, there were some gracious souls whose bitter anguish sought vent in wailing and lamentations—fit music to accompany that march of woe. When my soul can, in imagination, see the Saviour bearing His cross to Calvary, she joins the godly women and weeps with them; for, indeed, there is true cause for grief—cause lying deeper than those mourning women thought. They bewailed innocence maltreated, goodness persecuted, love bleeding, meekness about to die; but my heart has a deeper and more bitter cause to mourn. My sins were the scourges which lacerated those blessed shoulders, and crowned with thorn those bleeding brows: my sins cried "Crucify Him! crucify Him!" and laid the cross upon His gracious shoulders. His being led forth to die is sorrow enough for one eternity: but my having been His murderer, is more, infinitely more, grief than one poor fountain of tears can express.

Why those women loved and wept it were not hard to guess: but they could not have had greater reasons for love and grief than my heart has. Nain's widow saw her son restored—but I myself have been raised to newness of life. Peter's wife's mother was cured of the fever—but I of the greater plague of sin. Out of Magdalene seven devils were cast—but a whole legion out of me. Mary and Martha were favoured with visits—but He dwells with me. His mother bare His body—but He is formed in me the hope of glory. In nothing behind the holy women in debt, let me not be behind them in gratitude or sorrow.

> *"Love and grief my heart dividing,*
> *With my tears His feet I'll lave—*
> *Constant still in heart abiding,*
> *Weep for Him who died to save."*

Saturday Evening

"The place, which is called Calvary."

LUKE 23:33

The hill of comfort is the hill of Calvary; the house of consolation is built with the wood of the cross; the temple of heavenly blessing is founded upon the riven rock—riven by the spear which pierced His side. No scene in sacred history ever gladdens the soul like Calvary's tragedy.

> *"Is it not strange, the darkest hour*
> *That ever dawned on sinful earth,*

Should touch the heart with softer power,
*   For comfort, than an angel's mirth?*
That to the Cross the mourner's eye should turn,
*   Sooner than where the stars of Bethlehem burn?"*

Light springs from the midday-midnight of Golgotha, and every herb of the field blooms sweetly beneath the shadow of the once accursed tree. In that place of thirst, grace hath dug a fountain which ever gusheth with waters pure as crystal, each drop capable of alleviating the woes of mankind. You who have had your seasons of conflict, will confess that it was not at Olivet that you ever found comfort, not on the hill of Sinai, nor on Tabor; but Gethsemane, Gabbatha, and Golgotha have been a means of comfort to you. The bitter herbs of Gethsemane have often taken away the bitters of your life; the scourge of Gabbatha has often scourged away your cares, and the groans of Calvary yields us comfort rare and rich. We never should have known Christ's love in all its heights and depths if He had not died; nor could we guess the Father's deep affection if He had not given His Son to die. The common mercies we enjoy all sing of love, just as the sea-shell, when we put it to our ears, whispers of the deep sea whence it came; but if we desire to hear the ocean itself, we must not look at everyday blessings, but at the transactions of the crucifixion. He who would know love, let him retire to Calvary and see the Man of sorrows die.

Sunday Morning

"The precious blood of Christ."

1 PETER 1:19

Standing at the foot of the cross, we see hands, and feet, and side, all distilling crimson streams of precious blood. It is "precious" because of its *redeeming* and *atoning efficacy.* By it the sins of Christ's people are atoned for; they are redeemed from under the law; they are reconciled to God, made one with Him. Christ's blood is also "precious" in its *cleansing power;* it "cleanseth from all sin." "Though your sins be as scarlet, they shall be as white as snow." Through Jesus' blood there is not a spot left upon any believer, no wrinkle nor any such thing remains. O precious blood, which makes us clean, removing the stains of abundant iniquity, and permitting us to stand accepted in the Beloved, notwithstanding the many ways in which we have rebelled against our God. The blood of Christ is likewise "precious" in its *preserving power.* We are safe from the destroying angel under the sprinkled blood. Remember it is *God's seeing* the blood which is the true reason for our being spared. Here is comfort for us when the eye of faith is dim, for God's eye is still the same. The blood of Christ is "precious" also in its *sanctifying influence.* The same blood which justifies by taking away sin, does in its after-action, quicken the new nature and lead it onward to subdue sin and to follow out the commands of God. There is no motive for holiness so great as that which streams from the veins of Jesus. And "precious," unspeakably precious, is this blood, because it has *an overcoming power.* It is written, "They overcame through the blood of the Lamb." How could they do otherwise? He who fights with the precious blood of Jesus, fights with a weapon which cannot know defeat. The blood of Jesus! sin dies at its presence, death ceases to be death: heaven's gates are opened. The blood of Jesus! we shall march on, conquering and to conquer, so long as we can trust its power!

Sunday Evening

"Him hath God exalted."

ACTS 5:31

Jesus, our Lord, once crucified, dead and buried, now sits upon the throne of glory. The highest place that heaven affords is His by undisputed right. It is sweet to remember that the exaltation of Christ in heaven is a *representative exaltation.* He is exalted at the Father's right hand, and though as Jehovah He had eminent glories, in which finite creatures cannot share, yet as the Mediator, the honours which Jesus wears in heaven are the heritage of all the saints. It is delightful to reflect how close is Christ's union with His people. We are actually one with Him; we are members of His body; and His exaltation is *our* exaltation. He will give us to sit upon His throne, even as He has overcome, and is set down with His Father on His throne; He has a crown, and He gives us crowns too; He has a throne, but He is not content with having a throne to Himself, on His right hand there must be His queen, arrayed in "gold of Ophir." He cannot be glorified without His bride. Look up, believer, to Jesus now; let the eye of your faith behold Him with many crowns upon His head; and remember that you will one day be like Him, when you shall see Him as He is; you shall not be so great as He is, you shall not be so divine, but still you shall, in a measure, share the same honours, and enjoy the same happiness and the same dignity which He possesses. Be content to live unknown for a little while, and to walk your weary way through the fields of poverty, or up the hills of affliction; for by-and-by you shall reign with Christ, for He has "made us kings and priests unto God, and we shall reign for ever and ever." Oh! wonderful thought for the children of God! We have Christ for our glorious representative in heaven's courts *now*, and soon He will come and receive us to Himself, to be with Him there, to behold His glory, and to share His joy.

RESURRECTION
CELEBRATION

Beyond Good Friday

Why do I dwell on the close-up
and the near-at-hand
like Your followers
who stood beneath the cross,
sure they had lost all?
Lord Jesus, give me the grace—
the faith—
to look beyond the immediate,
believing that in spite of what I see,
Your power
is still available for me.
Praise God! You are risen!

—Lois Walfrid Johnson
Songs for Silent Moments

Were You There?

Were you there when they crucified my Lord?
Were you there when they crucified my Lord?
> Were you there when they nailed Him to the
> tree?
> Were you there when they nailed Him to the
> tree?
Were you there when they pierced Him in the side?
Were you there when they pierced Him in the side?
> Were you there when the sun refused to shine?
> Were you there when the sun refused to shine?
Were you there when they laid Him in the tomb?
Were you there when they laid Him in the tomb?

CHORUS
Oh! Sometimes it causes me to tremble, tremble,
> tremble,
Were you there when they crucified my Lord?

Were you there when He rose up from the grave?
Were you there when He rose up from the grave?

CHORUS
Oh! Sometimes I feel like shouting, Glory! Glory!
> Glory!
Were you there when He rose up from the grave?

—Traditional Spiritual

Low in the Grave He Lay

Low in the grave He lay, Jesus my Savior,
Waiting the coming day, Jesus my Lord!

Up from the grave He arose,
With a mighty triumph over His foes,
He arose a Victor from the dark domain,
And He lives forever, with His saints to reign.
He arose! He arose!
Hallelujah! Christ arose!

Vainly they watch His bed, Jesus my Savior;
Vainly they seal the dead, Jesus my Lord!

Death cannot keep its Prey, Jesus my Savior;
He tore the bars away, Jesus my Lord!

—Robert Lowry

He Lives

I serve a risen Savior, He's in the world today;
I know that He is living, whatever men may say;
I see His hand of mercy, I hear his voice of cheer,
And just the time I need Him, He's always near.

In all the world around me I see His loving care,
And tho' my heart grows weary I never will despair;
I know that He is leading thro' all the stormy blast,
The day of His appearing will come at last.

Rejoice, rejoice, O Christian,
    lift up your voice and sing
Eternal hallelujahs to Jesus Christ the King!
The Hope of all who seek Him,
    the Help of all who find,
None other is so loving, so good and kind.

CHORUS
He lives, He lives, Christ Jesus lives today!
He walks with me and talks with me along life's
    narrow way.
He lives, He lives, salvation to impart!
You ask me how I know He lives?
He lives within my heart.

                —A. H. Ackley

Joy Dawned Again
on Easter Day

Joy dawned again on Easter Day,
The sun shone out with fairer ray,
When, to their longing eyes restored
The Apostles saw their risen Lord.
O Jesus, King of gentleness,
Do Thou our inmost hearts possess;
And we to Thee will ever raise
The tribute of our grateful praise.
Jesus Who art the Lord of all,
In this our Easter festival
From every weapon death can wield
Thine own redeemed, Thy people, shield.
All praise, O risen Lord, we give
To Thee, Who dead, again dost live;
To God the Father equal praise,
And God the Holy Ghost, we raise.

—John Mason Neale

We Welcome Glad Easter

We welcome glad Easter when Jesus arose,
And won a great victory over His foes.

Then raise your glad voices, all Christians and sing,
Bring glad Easter tidings to Jesus, your King.

We tell how the women came early that day,
And there at the tomb found the stone rolled away.

We sing of the angel who said: "Do not fear!
Your Savior is risen, and He is not here."

We think of the promise which Jesus did give:
"That he who believes in Me also shall live!"

—Anonymous

Jesus Lives!

Jesus lives! no longer now
Can thy terrors, death, appall us;
Jesus lives! by this we know
Thou, O grave, canst not enthrall us.
Alleluia!

Jesus lives! henceforth is death
But the gate of life immortal;
This shall calm our trembling breath,
When we pass its gloomy portal.
Alleluia!

Jesus lives! for us He died;
Then, alone to Jesus living
Pure in heart may abide,
Glory to our Savior giving.
Alleluia!

Jesus lives! our hearts know well
Naught from us His love shall sever;
Life, nor death, nor powers of hell
Tear us from His keeping ever.
Alleluia!

Jesus lives! to Him the throne
Over all the world is given;
May we go where He is gone,
Rest and reign with Him in heaven.
Alleluia!

— Christian Gellert

Jesus Christ Is Risen Today

Jesus Christ is risen today, Alleluia!
Our triumphant holy day, Alleluia!
Who did once, upon the cross, Alleluia!
Suffer to redeem our loss, Alleluia!

Hymns of praise then let us sing, Alleluia!
Unto Christ, our heavenly King, Alleluia!
Who endured the cross and grave, Alleluia!
Sinners to redeem and save, Alleluia!

Sing we to our God above, Alleluia!
Praise eternal as His love, Alleluia!
Praise Him, all you heavenly host, Alleluia!
Father, Son, and Holy Ghost.

—Bohemian Carol

Ere Yet the Dawn Has Filled the Skies

Ere yet the dawn has filled the skies,
Behold, my Savior Christ arise;
He chaseth from us sin and night,
And brings us joy and life and light.
O stronger Thou than death and hell!
Where is the foe Thou canst not quell,
What heavy stone Thou canst not roll
From off the prisoned, anguished soul?
If Jesus lives, can I be sad?
I know He loves me, and am glad;
Though all the world were dead to me,
Enough, O Christ, if I have Thee!
He feeds me, comforts and defends,
And when I die His angel sends
To bear me whither He is gone,
For of His own He loseth none.
Strong Champion! For this comfort, see,
The whole world brings her thanks to Thee;
And once we, too, shall raise above
More sweet and loud the song of love.

—Johann Heerman

Hallelujah! Jesus Lives

Hallelujah! Jesus lives!
He is now the Living One;
From the gloomy halls of death
Christ, the conqueror, has gone,
Bright forerunner to the skies
Of His people, yet to rise.
Jesus lives! Why do you weep?
Why that sad and mournful sigh?
He who died our Brother here
Lives our Brother still on high.
Lives forever to bestow
Blessings on His church below.
Jesus lives! And thus, my soul,
Life eternal waits for you;
Joined to Him, your living head,
Where He is, you shall be, too;
With the Lord, at His right hand,
As a victor you shall stand.
Jesus lives! Let all rejoice.
Praise Him, ransomed of the earth.
Praise Him in a nobler song,
Cherubim of heavenly birth.
Praise the victor King, Whose sway
Sin and death and hell obey.
Hallelujah! Angels, sing!
—Carl Bernhard Garve

CHRIST IS RISEN!
HE IS RISEN INDEED!

The first day of the week cometh Mary Magdalene early, when it was yet dark, unto the sepulchre, and seeth the stone taken away from the sepulchre. . . . And they [the angels] say unto her, Woman, why weepest thou? She saith unto them, Because they have taken away my Lord, and I know not where they have laid him. And when she had thus said, she turned herself back, and saw Jesus standing, and knew not that it was Jesus. . . . Jesus saith unto her, Mary. She turned herself, and saith unto him, Rabboni; which is to say, Master (John 20:1, 13–14, 16).

One Easter

Joyfully, this Easter day,
I kneel, a little child, to pray;
Jesus, who hath conquered death,
Teach me, with my every breath,
To praise and worship Thee.
—Sharon Banigan

Although many have attempted to discredit the Resurrection, it has been authenticated by many witnesses including Matthew, Mark, John, and others enumerated by the apostle Paul.

> For I delivered unto you first of all that which I also received, how that Christ died for our sins according to the scriptures; And that he was buried, and that he rose again the third day according to the scriptures: And that he was seen of Cephas, then of the twelve: After that, he was seen of above five hundred brethren at once; of whom the greater part remain unto this present, but some are fallen asleep. After that, he was seen of James; then of all the apostles. And last of all he was seen of me also, as of one born out of due time.
>
> 1 Corinthians 15:3–8

Because people in the days of Paul were saying Christ had not risen from the dead, he refuted their arguments by following the premise to its logical end: "But if there be no resurrection of the dead, then is Christ not risen. . .then is our preaching vain, and your faith is also vain. . . . Ye are yet in your sins" (1 Corinthians 15:13–14, 17). Without the Resurrection, we would have no hope, either in this life nor in the life to come. Christ's Resurrection is the pivotal tenet of Christianity.

An extrabiblical, reliable authority concerning the Resurrection is Flavius Josephus. Josephus was a Jewish historian from Jerusalem, who was born around A.D. 33. In his account, Josephus notes:

Now there was about this time Jesus, a wise man, if it be lawful to call him a man; for he was a doer of wonderful works, a teacher of such men as receive the truth with pleasure. He drew over to him both many of the Jews and many of the Gentiles. He was [the] Christ. And when Pilate, at the suggestion of the principal men amongst us, had condemned him to the cross, those that loved him at the first did not forsake him; for he appeared to them alive again the third day; as the divine prophets had foretold these and ten thousand other wonderful things concerning him. And the tribe of Christians, so named from him, are not extinct at this day.

Blessed be the God and Father
of our Lord Jesus Christ,
which according to his abundant mercy
hath begotten us again unto a lively hope
by the resurrection of Jesus Christ from
the dead,
To an inheritance incorruptible, and unde-
filed, and that fadeth not away, reserved in
heaven for you,
Who are kept by the power of God
through faith unto salvation ready to be
revealed in the last time.

1 Peter 1:3–5

We've prepared for, meditated upon, and celebrated this most meaningful season. Now, before
we part, I extend my hand to you and with joyous
conviction declare, "He is risen." By faith, I feel the
warmth of your handclasp and hear your radiant
reply, "He is risen, indeed!"

Sense the awe. Anticipate the hope. Experience
the joy.

Inspirational Library

Beautiful purse/pocket-size editions of Christian classics
bound in flexible leatherette. These books make thoughtful
gifts for everyone on your list, including yourself!

When I'm on My Knees   The highly popular
collection of devotional thoughts on prayer,
especially for women.
Flexible Leatherette $4.97

The Bible Promise Book   Over 1000 prom-
ises from God's Word arranged by topic. What
does God promise about matters like: Anger,
Illness, Jealousy, Love, Money, Old Age, and
Mercy? Find out in this book!
Flexible Leatherette $3.97

Daily Wisdom for Women   A daily devotional
for women seeking biblical wisdom to apply to
their lives. Scripture taken from the New
American Standard Version of the Bible.
Flexible Leatherette $4.97

My Daily Prayer Journal   Each page is dated
and features a Scripture verse and ample room
for you to record your thoughts, prayers, and
praises. One page for each day of the year.
Flexible Leatherette $4.97

Available wherever books are sold.
Or order from:

Barbour Publishing, Inc.
P.O. Box 719
Uhrichsville, OH 44683
http://www.barbourbooks.com

If you order by mail add $2.00 to your order for shipping.
Prices subject to change without notice.